How to Talk Dirty

Talking Dirty Expert Sex Guide for Women with 200 Dirty Talk Examples

Includes Talk Dirty Tips to seduce your man

in bed, online, text, phone, phrases, and sex toys.

By

DK Overbaker

Published by Overbaker Publishing 2014

The accuracy and completeness of information provided herein and opinions stated herein are not guaranteed or warranted to produce any particular results and the advice and strategies, contained herein may not be suitable for every individual. The author shall not be liable for any loss incurred as a consequence of the use and application, directly or indirectly, of any information presented in this work. This publication is designed to provide information in regards to the subject matter covered.

About the Author

DK Overbaker is highly passionate about empowering women to take control of their love life. When she is not writing she loves swimming, jogging and travelling to exotic places.

Remember to subscribe to my newsletter so that I can send you regular dirty talk tips and general advice on keeping the romance in your relationship.

My website blog address is given below:

http://www.talkingdirtytoyourman.com/blog

Simply enter your name and email in the "Subscribe to our Newsletter" opt in box and I will send you regular dirty talk tips!

If you subscribe to my newsletter I will also send you a further 100 dirty talk examples!

Please Leave a **Review** after you have finished reading this book:

I would be very grateful if you could please take a moment to leave a good review for this guide. Tell me what you learnt from this guide after you have read it.

You can go to the Amazon page

http://www.amazon.com/How-Talk-Dirty-Talking-Examples-ebook/dp/B00JLZDU70

Once you are there click on "Write a review". I will be forever in your debt!

--DK Overbaker

Table of Contents

Chapter One: Introduction

"There's nothing better than a pretty girl with a filthy mouth.

That's every guy's fantasy."

Justin Timberlake (Singer and Film Star)

You are reading this book because you want to learn how to talk dirty. The quote displayed above is a secret fantasy of lots of guys. Justin Timberlake needs no introduction. He is a cutie who says that he likes girls talking dirty. If I happen to meet him I will definitely not say no if he wants to talk dirty. LOL!

My guess is that you are already in a relationship and want to add that extra spice to your sex life. Do you like to be the good girl on the street but talk dirty and act like a freak between the sheets? What better way than to seduce your man with those lovely dirty words. He will love you for it and he will keep begging you for more. My goodness dirty talking makes sex fantastic and my orgasms much more intense!

Talking dirty is such a powerful love tonic. Don't you just love the tingle you get when someone you like talks dirty to you? Your heart starts beating faster and you start blushing! Before the days of online cybersex and sex chat rooms some women posted messages on Craigslist. In those messages they usually asked men to write them back with dirty fantasies of what would happen when they meet.

Entire genres of music and porn are devoted to talking dirty. Visit a nightclub and it is likely you will hear music with dirty lyrics. Do you feel wonderful when you are enjoying some sensual music while dancing with your lover? How about when your man whispers all those sweet nothings into your ear while you bump and grind on the dance floor? Do you get goose pimples when he talks seductively to you on the phone?

So why is dirty talk so important? The truth is however strong a love relationship you have with your man, you are bound to go through some rough patches. Additionally your sexual relationship could become too dull and predictable.

During these rough patches you may feel as if you are just going through the motions without any passion and satisfaction. You do not look forward to your bedroom action like you used to when you were dating. Your relationship becomes too comfortable and you both start taking each other for granted. Your heart screams for passion and excitement but instead you feel numb and cannot figure out the reason you feel this way.

Worse you feel guilty because you do not want to burden your man with your fears. You do not know what to say to him. Of course you still love him. He has always been there for you and has always been dependable. You feel you should be thankful that you are still together especially when your best friend spends hours crying on your shoulders saying what a douchebag some men can be.

However you cannot get over the feeling that you want something to happen to help you escape your feeling of despair. As an escape you immerse yourself in your favorite romantic novel. Here you can transport yourself to a world where all your fantasies are satisfied.

Your loins seem to melt when the lover in your exotic book talks dirty to his girl and you feel a sense of excitement. You even imagine that you are the girl in the book. During your spare time you daydream and replay the images from your novel in your mind. These images make you realize that you want to make things hotter in bed. However you do not have the courage to ask your man how he feels about talking dirty. You feel embarrassed even thinking about it.

In particular you dread the thought that he would think you are a slut if you even gathered the courage to introduce such a topic to him. The truth is that you've had a strict upbringing and have always been taught that it is not the woman's place to take the lead in a sexual relationship. As a result you are not sure if you should shock your partner with your demands. After all society expects that nice girls should not entertain such dirty thoughts!

So why am I writing this book? The main reason is that the feelings and events described above happened at a certain time in my life. I was the girl who went through those experiences. Even before this I had some horrible experiences as a timid 19 year old teenager. My first boyfriend dumped me because he said I was not sexy enough. He said I did not do the things he liked when we made love. I was very hurt because I felt that he was the one for me.

It was such a terrible time. I felt as if my world had come to an end. I ballooned up in weight as I started to binge eat. The worst part was that I completely lost my confidence. It took a long time before I felt I was ready to pick up the pieces of my life. Indeed I am heavily indebted to my girlfriends who helped pull me through my agony. As a result I vowed that never again would I feel so low about myself.

To learn to be confident again I started exercising and paid more attention to my nutrition. As the months passed by my weight dropped and I started feeling more confident. I also started going out a lot more and mixing with lots of people.

Over the years my confidence in myself has been transferred to my sex life. I have become a better lover. Best of all I have mastered how to talk dirty and I'm not afraid to express my needs in bed. The language of lust is such a beautiful language. Your man will love you for it.

Hey I am here to help and guide you. Let me take you by the hand and teach you how to talk dirty and act like that wench in your favorite romantic novel. Your man would not be able to keep his hands off the dirty talking and sexy girl who you have become!

I will also provide you with tips to improve your sexual health. More importantly, you will become an expert dirty talker by the end of our journey and take your relationship with your man to a new level. This is the reason why you should learn how to talk dirty.

Why You Should Read This Book

You should read this book because it covers everything you need to know about talking dirty to your man. At the same time it is just not another dirty talk book. This book also teaches you about your female sexual body in a way that is easy to understand.

The resource section is priceless and includes information on different sex toys for masturbation. It also contains adult sex shop addresses in some popular cities around the world. The dirty talk toolbox in the resource section will include G-spot and squirting tips.

Furthermore you will also find information on sex toy care, Kegel exercises and the female sexual anatomy in the Resources section.

By the time you finish the book, you will become a confident and more knowledgeable lover who is not afraid to express herself in your bedroom. You will also gain more knowledge about your body and your female sexual anatomy.

What makes this book such a fantastic guide compared to other talk dirty books is the detailed **action steps** that you can carry out while you read.

Carrying out these action steps help you become an expert at talking dirty. You should be willing to carry out these steps if you want to get the full benefits of this book. I will not feel that I have helped you learn how to talk dirty if you do not practice these action steps.

Who Should Read This Book

You should read this book if:

You will like to talk dirty but do not know how to start.

You want to achieve more intimacy in your relationship with your man.

You want to learn to tell your man what you want in bed.

You are not sure of what type of dirty talk phrases to use.

You want to bring back your fire and passion in your bedroom

You want to unleash the sexual animal inside you and get in touch with your inner sex goddess.

Your man wants you to talk dirty in bed but you do not know what to say.

You need some more experience on using dirty talk phrases.

You have had a bad experience when talking dirty in a previous relationship.

You are afraid that your man will think you are a nasty girl if you talk dirty but you still want to learn.

You want to spice things up in your bedroom.

You will like to increase your dirty talk vocabulary skills in your bedroom.

You will like to learn how to talk dirty without feeling ashamed.

You are not sure of what kind of language to use when talking dirty.

You are afraid of saying the wrong things to your guy when you talk dirty.

You are shy but will like to learn to talk dirty in bed without being tongue tied.

You are having problems keeping your sex life hot and steamy.

You want to use dirty talk as a form of foreplay and role-play.

You will like to learn how to talk dirty naturally without looking ridiculous.

You want to be more vocal in your bedroom.

What You Are Going to Learn

A lot of women will like to learn how to talk dirty but do not know where to start. I used to be shy and afraid to express myself in bed. Indeed if the truth be told I was not the assertive type in any part of my life. As a result I got into lots of bad relationships in which the men in my life used me and dumped me.

First of all you will learn how to be comfortable about yourself. How else are you going to learn how to talk dirty if you are not confident?

I will then show you how to get you comfortable with your body through masturbating. Of course this is important because if you are not comfortable with your body you will find it difficult to role-play while talking dirty to your man. You will learn to find your G-spot. Once you find your G-spot I will also show you a masturbation technique to stimulate G-spot so that you can squirt. And yes squirting does exist although some women have never had the pleasure of having one.

After you have mastered how to squirt I will explain why your sexual fantasies play a very important role in improving your dirty talk skills. Imagining these sexual role-plays will help you become a better dirty talker. Furthermore I will provide you with examples of some sexual fantasies that are frequently imagined by women when they masturbate and dirty talk. These fantasies are imagined by many more women than you would think.

Next you will learn the language of dirty talk. Here you will identify your reasons for wanting to talk dirty. Knowing your reasons for wanting to talk dirty will make it easier for you to learn how to talk dirty. It will help you decide if you are comfortable with being a soft core or hardcore dirty talker.

First you will learn how to start talking dirty if you have never done it before. After this you will learn how to get your man in the mood outside your bedroom. Subsequently you will find out how to get your man in the mood in your bedroom and home.

Additionally you will also find out how to get yourself in the mood. Next you will find out how to start talking dirty in bed. In the last part of this section you will learn how to handle situations in bed where you feel uncomfortable with your partner's dirty talk.

Once you have finished all I have discussed above you will move on to the chapter about Sexting. You will find out why it is one of your most powerful tools for dirty talk. You will also find out the dangers to avoid during Sexting.

After this you will move on to the chapter on phone sex. I will tell you why you should use phone sex as a way of maintaining a long distance relationship.

Next you will move on to the cybersex and sex chat room chapter. Cybersex and sex chat rooms are advanced dirty talk techniques. In particular you will learn about what goes on in cybersex and sex chat rooms. You will also find out about the benefits and dangers of cybersex.

You will discover what BDSM means and some of the sexual role-play activities that take place during BDSM. Of course BDSM is an advanced dirty talking activity.

Best of all I have provided you with 200 dirty talk examples which you can use to practice your dirty talk. These phrases are exclusively for women and have been used by them during masturbation or sex. You will find these dirty talk phrases towards the end of the book.

I have even included some dirty terms you can use to increase your dirty talk vocabulary.

Throughout the book you will find action steps to help you improve your dirty talk skills. These action steps are extremely important. They will help you practice what you have read in this book.

By the time you finish reading this book you will become very comfortable talking dirty to your partner both outside and inside your bedroom, during phone sex, during Sexting, Cybersex or in sex chat rooms.

I have included a resource guide at the end of the book. The resource guide contains lots of useful information. This includes the addresses of adult sex shops in a number of major cities. In addition you will learn about your female sexual anatomy. By knowing more about your sexual organs you will learn what turns you on. Learning about your sexual anatomy also teaches you how to improve your sexual health.

In addition you will also find out about Kegel exercises. These exercises help you tone your pelvic muscles for better squirting. In the resource guide you will also find out the names of some popular sex toys that you can use for masturbation and dirty talking. Make sure you practice your dirty talk while using these toys on yourself and your partner.

When you finish and have practiced the tips in this book, you will have found out a lot more about your sexual self. With your new knowledge, you will definitely enjoy a better relationship with your guy.

Chapter Two: Getting Comfortable with Who You Are

Before you can learn how to talk dirty you first have to learn to be comfortable with yourself. Learning how to talk dirty is a whole new language. You have to be able to talk about what you are going to do to your body and your lover's body without feeling ashamed.

I used to be very shy and timid. I was also very ashamed of my body. The worst part was that all my boyfriends used to treat me like trash. I was afraid to tell them what I wanted from our relationship. It used to be that they take, take, take and not give anything worthwhile in return. All that changed when I decided that it was time for me to take back control of my life.

Building up your self esteem is a fantastic way to get comfortable with yourself. You need to be confident and have high self esteem to be able to talk dirty.

You have probably heard the saying "a sound mind in a sound body." Keeping fit and healthy is a brilliant way to learn to build your self esteem. Start some form of exercise if you feel unfit and overweight. You can exercise at home or at a gym. You could even go for a swim. I love swimming and swim almost every day.

Also pay attention to your nutrition and learn to eat the right foods for your body. Exercising and eating the right foods will make you look good and feel good! You will also be in great health which is a fantastic way to build up your self esteem.

I also use hypnosis as a way to build up my confidence and self esteem. The reason I enjoy hypnosis is because it helps me achieve an altered state of mind. I especially like "Conversational Hypnosis" because it helps make me more happy and enjoyable around people. Conversational hypnosis will help you acquire the skills needed to engage people in difficult conversations. You can pick up a good conversational hypnosis books in any major bookshop or on Amazon.

What is the next step you take in getting comfortable with your body?

The answer to this comes in one word.

Masturbation!

Yeah I said it. You have to be comfortable with masturbating.

The fact is your parents gave birth to you after they had sex. If you were a test tube baby, then it means you were born from masturbation. So tell me. Why should you be ashamed of masturbating or talking about sex? You should stop thinking of sex as a shameful and taboo subject. Instead embrace it as an enjoyable experience and a vital and natural part of your life.

You have to get to know your own body. Masturbation will make you realize what you like. If you do not know what you like how can someone else know? You definitely have to fall in love with your body and know what takes you to the highest points of ecstasy. If you love your body you will be able to talk about it to your lover and tell him what you want. When you both open up to each other by talking your relationship will grow and become more intimate. The more relaxed you become about your sexuality, the more likely you are to embrace dirty talk.

How do you build your self esteem to talk dirty in a sexy way? To build your self esteem to talk dirty you have to practice, practice, and practice. The more you masturbate the better your chances of discovering all your erogenous zones. Discovering your erogenous zones will definitely heighten your dirty talk pleasure.

The more you have sex with yourself the better you will be at having sex with your partner. Masturbating for your partner is a big turn-on. You can both practice mutual masturbation when you are both comfortable. Believe me men get excited seeing you masturbating while moaning and talking dirty at the same time. Your relationship will become more intimate as you both drop your inhibitions.

Make sure you practice masturbation. Masturbating gives you the chance to explore your sexual fantasies. All you need to do is to let go of your feelings of shame and embarrassment so that you can become more comfortable with your body. Get to know your own body. Enjoy getting to know yourself. You will learn more about masturbation in the next chapter.

Action Step

Write down what you will like to change about your body and love life. What are your insecurities? What are you going to do to change your insecurities?

Chapter Three: Masturbation

I started masturbating at a very early age. It was something that I did to relive myself at night. As I got older I remember feeling ashamed about it. I felt that I was a horrible person who was doing something disgusting. I tried to stop myself from masturbating. It was no use. I could not stop.

This shame persisted until when I got older. It was then that I was able to talk about sex with my friends. Some of them also admitted that they masturbated. I was so relieved to find out that I was not alone. I only wish that someone could have told me earlier that there was nothing wrong with my masturbating during my preteen years. It would have saved me a guilty conscience. I guess it is something parents do not wish to talk about.

Masturbation was such a taboo subject when I was growing up. Good girls were not supposed to masturbate. Instead it was supposed to be a normal activity for men. Little wonder that some girls suffered penis envy.

My experience grew from cucumbers and electric toothbrushes to dildos and vibrators. The list of objects that I used to practice masturbation was endless. I was not afraid to experiment and as I got older I grew more adventurous.

I discovered how to touch myself all over my body as I masturbated. I stroked my nipples, clitoris, vagina and anus while masturbating. I also found out that my excitement intensified if I fantasized and talked dirty during masturbation. I read erotic literature before masturbating, to give myself ideas. I read both simple and hard core erotica. Whatever kind of erotica I choose to read depended on my mood at that moment.

You are the only one that knows what satisfies you sexually. Now is the best time to find out if you are unsure. You can use solo masturbation to find out what turns you.

Once you are comfortable and confident about masturbating you can practice mutual masturbation with your partner. Your relationship becomes more intimate as you both drop your inhibitions.

Make time for masturbation because it helps you dig into your fantasies and pleasures. You also become more aware of your own female sexuality. Practicing masturbation helps you become more confident about your body. This increased self assurance will help you become more confident about talking dirty to your man.

Moreover you benefit from regular masturbation because it gives you a greater chance of locating your G-spot!

Where Is Your G-spot?

The G-spot is named after the German gynaecologist Ernest Grafenberg. It is the source of female squirting.

Your G-spot is the sensitive area around the front of the vagina. It is between 2.5cm to 3.5cm inside your vagina and close to the pubic bone. Your urethral sponge is located behind it. This is the reason you sometimes feel like you want to pee while pleasuring your G-spot. At the point of orgasm some women expel some fluid from their urethra. Your G-spot is easier to find when you are aroused. Using sex toys on your G-spot when aroused while talking dirty will heighten your pleasure. You can also ask your partner to stimulate your G-spot with sex toys.

Learning about your G-spot is one of the first moves towards understanding what turns your body on. It builds up your knowledge of your erogenous zones and pleasure spots.

What Does a G-spot Orgasm or Squirting Feel Like

Your urethral sponge is behind your G-spot. When you stimulate your G-spot with your fingers you are actually applying pressure to your urethral sponge. Your urethral sponge is in your urethra and is the organ through which urine passes out of your body. Since your urethral sponge is part of your urethra you may sometimes feel the urge to pee when you stroke your G-spot. If you continue stimulating your G-spot with your fingers long enough you may ejaculate through your urethra. This is what is known as the famous squirting!

A G-spot orgasm feels like a whole body experience. It is a much deeper orgasm than a clitoral orgasm. Sometimes you feel contractions in your vaginal walls from G-spot orgasms. Most of our orgasms come from clitoral stimulation and most women discover vaginal orgasms by accident rather than by intent. Get to know you're G-spot and you will be introduced to a world of earth shattering masturbation pleasure.

Masturbating Your G-spot

The great boxing ring announcer Michael Buffer usually says this whenever he introduces two undefeated boxers. He says "Someone's O has got to go." Well with the techniques you will learn here your O (orgasm) has definitely got to go. LOL! You will learn to have an orgasm even though we are not talking about boxers. That is unless you have a boxing fetish. Let's get ready to rumble!

Here is how you masturbate your G-spot.

Put your fingers inside your vagina and check for the sensitive spot close to the front of your vaginal wall. Your G-spot feels slightly spongy.

Begin stroking the spot with your fingers.

As you continue stroking this spot it will start to swell.

Keep on stroking it. You need to apply constant and strong pressure. Not too firm or too swift. You can also use a sex toy specially designed to reach your G-spot. It is much easier to stimulate your G-spot with the toy.

For added pleasure you can also stimulate your clitoris at the same time.

Keep on titillating your G-spot. It will continue to swell and you might hear a splashing sound.

Continue going. You might start feeling the urge to pee. Just make sure you stay relaxed. Don't tense your pelvic muscles.

Once you feel the urge to pee you will know that you might be about to squirt.

Keep going until you squirt.

Action Step

When you are alone in bed get relaxed and explore your body to find out your erogenous zones. Once you are aroused insert your fingers into your vagina and begin masturbating. Stroke the sensitive area around your vagina to try to find your G-spot. Remember to be patient and relaxed and try talking dirty to yourself. By being relaxed you stand a better chance of finding your G-spot and enjoying a good squirt!

.

Chapter Four: Sexual Fantasy

In this section you will learn why your sexual fantasies are crucial in helping you learn to talk dirty. This is one of the most important sections of this book. Maybe you are asking yourself what is my reason for saying this section is so important? There is a simple answer. Your sexual fantasies play a big part in what you say when you talk dirty. Before you can learn how to talk dirty you have to think dirty.

Did you know that around 80 percent of your sex life takes place in your head even before you actually make love? Some women actually think their sexual fantasies are more intimate than love making. We spend more time thinking about sex than doing it.

Sex does indeed start in the brain and this is why our fantasies give us so much pleasurable feelings.

One of the reasons that we talk dirty is to arouse our sexual fantasies. Stirring up your sexual fantasies and dirty talking at the same time can be a very powerful sexual foreplay technique. The more you fantasize, the easier it is for you to talk dirty during sex. Indeed your sexual fantasies can be your greatest foreplay to get you in the mood.

I frequently fantasize about what myself and my man will do to each other in bed. Even if your lover is the greatest fuck in the world it still helps to fantasize. You do not really know your lover until you know their fantasies. Once you can both share your fantasies with each other your relationship will grow.

I also love to fantasize while masturbating. For me masturbation without fantasy is not exciting. At times I talk dirty and fantasize about my man when I am masturbating. Other times I fantasize about having sex with a gorgeous film star. This is just one of my fantasies.

My sexual fantasies are a form of sexual foreplay and excitement. Sometimes during foreplay with my guy my favourite fantasies pop up in my head. This gets me even more excited. I know that some of you might be shocked. Does it really matter what I think during sex if it excites me. When I am in that mood it makes my man horny and enriches our love life.

One of the greatest difficulties as a female is telling your fantasies to your man. It does not matter how wild your fantasy seem to you. As far as it makes you happy it's okay. You should not be afraid to acknowledge your fantasies to your man. However do not reveal your fantasies if you feel that your man would get hurt.

One way that I fulfil my dirty talk and sexual fantasies is through role-play. I love to role-play. While role-playing you can pretend that you and your partner are someone else. Maybe you fancy playing the role of a nurse, French maid, bunny girl, or a dirty talking school teacher. On the other hand you may want your man to play the role of a fireman, sexy marine, construction worker or horny gynaecologist. The best thing about role-play is you can fulfil your fantasies without harming anyone.

My sexual fantasies and dirty talk are very important to me when I make love. Indeed it gets my heart beating faster and I get very excited to hear my man talk dirty. I get turned on by words like shagging, bashing, screwing and balling.

It is no surprise that some of these words also occur in my sexual fantasies while masturbating I get into a frenzy thinking about words like boobs, knockers, tart, pecker, dong, shaft, plunge and fellatio. This is why I love reading erotic fiction. It helps me increase my dirty talk vocabulary and gets me in the mood for lovemaking.

Here are some of the fantasies shared by my female friends.

Examples of Sexual Fantasies Shared by My Friends

Enjoy sex with a group of black men.

Have sex with another girl alone on a sunny beach

Enjoy threesome sex with a lesbian and a male stranger.

Wear a strap-on penis and fuck my boyfriend with it.

Watch my man fucking one of my girlfriends.

Have threesome sex with her boyfriend and another man.

Enjoy interracial sex with another girl.

Have sex with a handsome big black guy who talks dirty.

Fantasize about making love to lots of girls during a lesbian sex party.

Fantasize about being a stripper and performing paid sexual favours.

Masturbate with a vibrator while she talks dirty and thinks of a man or girl she saw on the street.

Kidnap and tie up a man and force him to give her oral sex whenever she desired.

Imagine she is a nurse who has sex with the well hung male patient during the night shift.

Have sex with a group of girls on her bedroom floor during a slumber party.

Fantasize about herself and her guy making love to multiple partners in a wife swap club.

Make love to her guy in a park while strangers watch them.

Tied up by a strange man and forced to do his bidding.

Fantasize about making love to a film star while masturbating.

Fantasize she reaches down a man's briefs on a crowded beach and masturbates his huge penis.

Fantasize about sleeping on a beach and waking up to find a tall blonde girl plunging her tongue into her hot wet pussy.

Take part in a sex party orgy.

She is a dominatrix who forces her boyfriend to obey all her sexual commands.

Fantasize about a master who forces her to obey all his sexual commands.

Her boyfriend gives her an oral while she goes down on another woman.

Tied up and blindfolded in the girls shower room while different girls grope her body and force her to give them oral sex.

Enjoy sex with an older woman while the woman's randy husband masturbates and watches them through the keyhole.

Have sex with a couple.

Have sex with an older man.

Fantasize about being a French maid who is forced to have sex with the master of the house.

Enjoy sex with her male doctor during a medical examination.

She is undressed, seduced and fucked by 5 girls during a bachelorette party.

She is the strict school mistress who punishes and shags the new male teacher for being rude.

Tied and bound by two elderly spinsters who use a dildo to fuck her in both ends.

She is unable to pay for her drinks in a bar and forced to have sex with the both the bar owner and all the male waiters.

She is caught and shagged by an escaping sex starved prisoner.

She enjoys a steamy love session with two black girls in a sauna.

Have a bubble bath and sex with a swinging couple in a Jacuzzi.

Fantasize about having sex with the beautiful female air hostess on the airplane.

She is spanked and forced to perform to perform oral sex on two waitresses for being rude to them.

Have fantasies about being dominated by a dominatrix.

Fantasize she is a cowgirl who is banged in the barn by the stable boy.

She is caught masturbating with the kitchen utensils and is punished by the chef.

Fantasize about having sex and a hot shower with a lovely brunette dyke.

She is a nurse who has sex with 2 male doctors during her work shift.

Fantasize she is a mistress who shags her man with a dildo and makes him do the housework.

She is the female doctor who has sex with the inmate during a prison call.

Caught stealing during maid duties and made to pay by satisfying her master's sex fetish desires.

Masturbate in schoolgirl uniform while the hidden dirty old male neighbour watches.

Fantasize about having an orgy with the entire college male swim team.

She enjoys a lesbian session with the strict elderly female librarian.

Why Your Sexual Fantasies Are Crucial in Helping You Learn to Talk Dirty

A study was carried out by researchers at the Department of Personality, Evaluation and Psychological Treatment (University of Granada, 2007). The researchers published some interesting information about sexual fantasies among women and men.

The researchers found out that among women, the more sexual fantasies they had, the more sexual desire they experienced. The researchers also found out that men respond more positively towards sexual stimuli and thoughts. Men had an attitude that together with sexual fantasies heightens sexual drive.

The researchers also stressed that education on sexual stimulation and response as well as healthy attitudes towards sexuality is extremely important. If people had healthy attitudes towards sexuality it would make sexual intercourse more pleasurable.

For me the above study highlights why your sexual fantasies play such an important role in increasing your sexual desire. Expressing your sexual fantasies and thoughts through dirty talk will definitely increase the sexual desires of both yourself and your guy. You should accept your partner's fantasies without being judgemental. It takes a lot of courage for them to reveal their hidden self to you. Encourage them to fulfil their sexual fantasies through dirty talk in a safe place. Dirty talk between couples is really another form of sexual expression and it will definitely make for a more trusting relationship.

Some of my girlfriends have told me how important it is to them to have their men talk dirty to them. They love hearing words like "my sexy little slut", bad girl," dirty little girl", "hot wet sexy pussy", "you horny wench" and "who is the daddy." Hearing these words in bed increased their libido. They also told me that their men loved it when they talked dirty. It spiced up things inside and outside their bedroom.

Action Step

Relax in bed and start masturbating with your favorite sex toys. As you masturbate think about your favorite fantasy. Think about your teenage and current sexual fantasies. Start talking dirty and experience all the feelings and sensations as if your fantasy is real. You can use some of the phrases in the talking dirty examples section of this book. The more you practice the more relaxed you will feel.

Chapter Five: Language of Dirty Talk

"All I really need to understand is when you talk dirty to me"

Jason Derulo (R & B star)

The above quote is from the Jason Derulo song "Talk dirty". It is a song about girls all over the world. The song explains that you do not need to understand your girl's language. All you really need to understand is when she talks dirty.

It's true. In my relationships with men I have found that they get highly turned on by the language of dirty talk. They just can't get enough of you. Yes they might dream of having a good girl to show their parents but they definitely want a naughty girl between the sheets!

Talking dirty is a very pleasurable adventure and can be a most potent aphrodisiac. It could be the tender sweet whisperings of endearments from the heart to your man or it could be just raw hungry possessive passion. Whichever it is, talking dirty should just feel natural to you. Sex without dirty talking is like driving to a place you have never been before without a GPS. Let's face it your car journey will be no fun. You will suffer lots of frustration without your dirty talk GPS!

Talking dirty gives you the chance to connect emotionally with your man. It takes your relationship to the next level because you learn to trust your guy with your fantasies. You are able to express yourself to your guy by telling him exactly what you want in bed.

Once you become skilled at dirty talk you will be able to coax your man to reveal their fantasies. If you do not know your lover's fantasies you do not really know him. Without dirty talk how are you ever going to find out what he really likes in bed? How he likes to be touched? What words he likes you to use? What role-plays he will like both of you to do together? How are you really going to find out what you both love to do together? To really become good at talking dirty you have to know your lover's sexual needs and fantasies. Ask him about his feelings, dreams, desires and needs.

Indeed women who converse about their sexual desires with their man have sex more frequently and are more orgasmic. Talking dirty to your man is one of the simplest ways to spice up your sex life. It is really easy to learn to talk dirty.

What Are Your Reasons for Wanting to Talk Dirty

Knowing your reasons for wanting to talk dirty will make it easier for you to learn to talk dirty. So what are your reasons? Is it any of the following given below.

You will like to talk dirty but do not know how to start.

You want to achieve more intimacy in your relationship with your man.

You want to learn to tell your man what you want in bed.

You are not sure of what type of dirty talk phrases to use.

You want to bring back your fire and passion in your bedroom

You want to unleash the sexual animal inside you and get in touch with your inner sex goddess.

Your man wants you to talk dirty in bed but you do not know what to say.

You need some more experience on using dirty talk phrases.

You have had a bad experience when talking dirty in a previous relationship.

You are afraid that your man will think you are a nasty girl if you talk dirty but you still want to learn.

You want to spice things up in your bedroom.

You will like to increase your dirty talk vocabulary skills in your bedroom.

You will like to learn how to talk dirty without feeling ashamed.

You are not sure of what kind of language to use when talking dirty.

You are afraid of saying the wrong things to your guy when you talk dirty.

You are shy but will like to learn to talk dirty in bed without being tongue tied.

You are having problems keeping your sex life hot and steamy.

You want to use dirty talk as a form of foreplay and role-play.

You will like to learn how to talk dirty naturally without looking ridiculous.

You want to be more vocal in your bedroom.

This book will certainly help you in your mission to become a better talker. Identify your reason for wanting to talk dirty and make the conscious decision to improve your dirty talking skills.

Many women feel very uncomfortable about talking dirty if they have never done it before. They are not sure how to introduce dirty talk into their love life. It is difficult for them because they do not know what to say or do.

This is because we have been told from childhood that it isn't right to speak that way. When we are in a relationship many of us are afraid to show our partner the real us because we feel that they will no longer respect us. Some guys are afraid of women who want to express their sexual desires. These men feel that they are cheap girls. That is so untrue. For me if a man feels that way I'd rather not bother about continuing a relationship with him.

So how do you start talking dirty if you have never done it before? I know you cannot become a hardcore dirty talker overnight. Start with some soft core dirty talk. This is simply as easy as telling your man how much you love him. Tell him how sexy he looks. Compliment him. The truth is that while men might like to act macho they actually like being complimented.

I was listening to a radio show recently. The female DJ announced she was going to reveal her list of the top 100 sexist men in the world during the next show. Before the next show most of the male DJs were very excited and were being very charming to the female DJ in an attempt to be included on the list.

However when the results were announced by the female DJ most of the male DJs were unhappy with their position on the top 100 chart. They even came on her show to complain that they were not happy with their position in the charts. And we think that men do not care about compliments and what their peers think about them!

Find out what turns your guy on. If you have already having sex then I am sure you already have some idea of what turns him on.

How about playing a sex game with him to find out his fantasies? You could also leave him a note telling him you love him and ask him to write and describe one of his fantasies so that you could both act it out. If he does not write a reply tease him in a playful way about it.

Continue leaving him notes describing how horny he makes you feel when you make love. Tell him how much he turns you on. Paint a clear picture of how much you desire him with your words. Make a listing of stuff that fires up your guy's lust and include them in your love notes. Also tell him that you want to make him very happy and will like to play out his fantasies.

Once he becomes more responsive to your love notes make them more passionate. Start making sultry phone calls to him in which you describe exactly how you are going to fulfil his fantasies. Also send him short sexy text messages with promises of what you have in store for him when you see him.

When your man is at work, call him while you are masturbating and describe the dirty things you will do to him when you meet. Include a scenario of his and your fantasies in your description of what you have in store for him during sex.

Make sure he hears your moans, groans and sighs of delight while you masturbate. This is guaranteed to get him hot and panting for you. He will have a picture of your hot sexy body in his mind. You can be sure that the last thing on his mind will be going out with the boys for a drink in the evening.

Use the masturbation and fantasy exercises in earlier chapters to improve your dirty talking skills. Find out what turns you on so that you can include them in your dirty talk. I am sure that by now you have made a diary of all your lusts and crushes from the exercises you completed in the earlier chapters. You will feel more comfortable adding these lusts and crushes into your dirty talk.

Make sure you use a sexy voice when talking to your man. This gets him quickly in the mood for sex later on. Make your voice as sultry and sexy as possible. When talking to your man lighten and modify your tone. This will make it easier for him to respond to you.

A sexy tone definitely gets your man all excited. Who hasn't heard of those sexy Swedish phone sex talks that used to get guys all horny and excited. . For me I get excited and turned on when I listen to the French language being spoken by an attractive French man. It is not as if I understand most of the words. What I enjoy most about spoken French is the tone the language is delivered.

The best way to learn how to sound sexy when talking dirty is to by practising in front of a mirror. Masturbate while you talk dirty. Do you feel relaxed and comfortable when you are alone and talking dirty? If you do not feel relaxed or your voice sounds strained then this is the right time to work on improving them.

Remember the things you both did during sex. What did he enjoy most? Imagine those things he loved you doing to him. Picture these with the most stunning and vivid imagination in your mind. Make sure you describe the things you imagine. Moan, sigh and breathe harder as you talk dirty. Pretend you are talking to your lover. You can also record your voice on your cell phone to find out how you sound while you practise jerking off in front of the mirror.

The more you practice the better you will become. You will become a more confident dirty talker. Dirty talk is not hard. All you are doing is telling your man how much you love him, how he makes you feel, and the things you will like both of you to do in bed.

The secret to learning to talk dirty is as simple as trying out things that you know your man will like. You know him better than anyone else. It is also important that you tell him what you want. A good way to do this is by engaging in playful conversation with him and drop hints about what you like to do when making love. This way he will not be surprised when you make certain demands in bed.

Talking dirty to your partner is all about using words that do not make you feel uncomfortable. How would you feel if your man used words like tart, hooker, slag, slut, tramp, wanton, bitch, hoe, or hussy? Now is the best time to find out. You should also read some erotica to help you enhance your dirty vocabulary.

Action Step

When you are alone, practice the dirty talk phrases you are comfortable using during your dirty talk. The most important thing here is that you feel at ease with using these phrases. They don't have to be hardcore dirty talk phrases.

How to Get Him in the Mood outside Your Home

You can engage in some foreplay long before you take your dirty talk into your bedroom. This can be as subtle as a heated glance filled with sexual intent in a public place. On the other hand it could be as bold as a scorching kiss in a secluded area of the park. As you kiss him you could whisper the dirty things that you have planned for both of you. I know that the look, the touches, the flirting, the wait and want will drive him wild.

A great place to practice your dirty talking skills on your man is in public places. Restaurants, cinemas, malls, amusement parks, the circus, stand-up comedy shows, carnivals, concerts, water parks, theme parks, and the beach are just some of the places for some naughty talk.

Suppose you are on the beach and you are riding water scooters with your man you could whisper to him that there is going to be a lot of riding and revving up tonight just like this scooter. All that naughty talk is sure to get his imagination fired up.

How about when you are lying down in the hot sand on the beach? You are wearing your favorite sexy swimwear which always turns him on. As he is rubbing some sun cream on you whisper to him that soon there will be no swimwear to prevent him from having his wicked way with you!

You could also engage in some dirty talk when dining with him in a restaurant. As you order some oysters you could innocently remark that you are looking forward to experiencing all its benefits later on. Alternatively you could order some ice cream for dessert and while you are eating it you could wink and tell him that it reminds you of something else that melts in your mouth.

You can direct your dirty talk to things they love about your body or clothing. Is he an ass man, leg man, breast man, or into fetish? If they are a breast man and it is a hot day you could say something like "Are you thirsty? I wish I could put some ice on my tits so that you could nibble them."

Men are sight beings. They respond to sexual images and sexual thoughts. Use this to your benefit by demonstrating what you are going to do to your guy with everyday objects around the house. Suppose your lover is doing some DIY at home. You could pick up and stroke the drill he is using for some repairs. Look him straight in the eye and wink while you say, "I like how long and hard this drill is, don't you?"

The beauty of dirty talk is that it allows you to be another person for a short while during your role-play. This can be quite liberating.

You can forget your everyday problems for a moment and immerse yourself in your sexual fantasies.

Whenever you are talking dirty to your man in a public place always remember that your dirty talk is for his ears only. Make sure friends do not hear the naughty things you say to him. After all you do not want him to feel embarrassed in front of his friends.

How to Get Him in the Mood inside Your Bedroom and Home

Lighten the Atmosphere around Your House

The last thing you want is a dirty and untidy house for your night of dirty talk. You want to make the atmosphere around the house as enchanting as possible. Be sure to clean and tidy up around the house. Change the bedding and replace them with clean and scented sheets. Get some soft lights to create some ambience. Order your favorite flowers to remind you of your favorite aroma. Remember to place these flowers all around your home. You can light up your fireplace if you have one. Do not forget your collection of his favorite music. Create a nice ambience around your home.

Make It a Romantic Night Just For Two

This is your night. There is nothing more frustrating than being disturbed by friends when you plan a night of unbridled passion. Make sure you tell your friends that you have plans for the night with your man and you will talk to them the next day. If you have children send them to their grandparents for the night. Yes I know you love your children and might feel guilty about sending them away. Taking a break from the kids for just one night will leave you refreshed and energised. It is better for your kids in the long run because they will have a happy mum. I am sure your kids do not want a stressed out mum who keeps scolding them.

Set Up Your House for Dinner by Candlelight

Nothing gets you in a better mood for a dirty talk love session than a romantic candlelight dinner at home. There is something so sexy about dinner by candlelight with some soft music playing in the background. After all music is the food of love. You do not even have to cook the meal yourself. You can order your guy's favorite meal from his favorite restaurant. It is said that the best way to a man's heart is by giving him good food. LOL!

Do not forget to buy his favorite wine to go with the meal. Serve the food and wine in your best plates and cutlery. Now is the time to display all your lovely china, wine glasses, silver cutlery and your favorite dinner table cloth! Make sure you both resist the urge to eat or drink too much. You do not want to both fall asleep immediately after dinner. After all the real fun begins after dinner!

Get Your Bathroom Ready for a Romantic Bath Together

This is the grand finale to get you in the mood for some dirty talking sex. Once you have built up the mood by having dinner you could both take a sexy bath together. It does not matter whether you have an ordinary bathtub or Jacuzzi. Make sure that you get the setting right. Light some scented candles. Remember to buy some large towels and sponges. Add some bath salts bubble bath to the water. Be sure to get your favorite champagne so that you can both sip it together while relaxing in the bath. After your bath you can massage each other's bodies with aromatherapy oils like lemon oil, peppermint oil, lavender, jasmine, chamomile, and sage oil. These oils will make you both feel relaxed and at peace with yourselves. Do not forget to have some music in the bathroom.

Buy Some Sexy Uniforms, Sexy lingerie and Perfume

How about some Victoria Secrets or Agent Provocateur lingerie or that perfume that he likes on you? How about a role-play outfit such as a saucy French maid, sexy school teacher, bunny girl, or a nurse outfit? This is your night to seduce him with your dirty talk. It is no secret that men get turned on by nice perfumes, sexy underwear and uniforms. You could even decorate your room to reflect your dressing. For example if you plan to get a nursing uniform you could also get a stethoscope and thermometer to decorate the room. It will give you a chance to check his temperature and heartbeat later on!

How to Get Yourself in the Mood

So how do you get yourself in the mood for a fantastic bout of dirty talk quality time with your man? Well it really depends on you. The most important thing is that you do whatever makes you feel relaxed and comfortable. Here are a few pointers to get you prepared:

Look into the mirror and tell yourself that you are the most beautiful and sexy woman in the world who will be able to drive any man wild with your dirty talk.

Visualise your favorite sex fantasies

Picture the most intimate sex sessions you had with your man.

Read an erotic or romantic book for some emotional stimulation. You can even read your old love letters.

Listen to your favorite music.

Take a beverage such as wine or herbal tea to relax. Make sure you do not take too much wine because you do not want to get drunk.

Watch an Erotic or Romantic Movie or Watch Some Porn

To get you in the mood how about a romantic film like
"Shakespeare in Love" with Gwyneth Paltrow?

Relive Your Best Sex Session

Remember the best hot and steamy sex you had with him. Did it
make you wet and horny? What turned you on most? How did
your body respond?

Use Aromatherapy to Get into the Mood

You can use scents like lavender and chamomile to help you relax.
Some scents offer an uprising sense of well-being while others
aromas can work as aphrodisiacs. You can also burn candles in a
softly lit bathroom while bathing in a tub of scented water and enjoy
the fragrance from all those lovely scents.

How to Start Talking Dirty in Bed

Sex without dirty talk and passion feels like a chore you quickly want
done so that you can do other things. Get him to share his fantasies
with you. When you are making love to him describe one of your
fantasies which you know will not shock him. Describe it to him so
vividly that he will get quite horny. Over time as you become more
confident you can begin to describe your wilder fantasies to him.

As soon as he opens up to you and tells you his fantasies you can
start talking seductively about them when you make love. During
your love making you describe how you are going to fulfil his
fantasies while you make love. This is guaranteed to turn him on.
The key to good dirty sex talk in bed is verbal communication and
trust. The best thing about dirty talk is that you get to learn much
more about your man.

Start with something as easy as a groan, moan or sigh when you feel pleasure during lovemaking. Find out what sounds turn your guy on by experimenting in bed. Some guys could get turned on just by the sound of your heavy breathing. Dirty talk in bed is all about going at your own pace and taking things as they come. From your guy's response you will be able to gauge if you should rev up your naughty talk.

Make sure that you describe his fantasies in a sexy and seductive voice. It is no secret that men can get turned on by a female voice. Your descriptions do not have to be in a loud and rough voice. In-fact you could say it in a soft and sultry voice. It's astonishing how something as simple as this can turn your man on. Include simple phrases like:

You are so good.

I love it when you do that.

You make me feel like a princess.

I have been thinking of getting this all day.

You make me feel so wonderful.

You are the best.

Your kiss takes me to the heights of ecstasy.

You make me feel so sexy.

"Yes! Yes! Yes!

Whisper the above sweet nothings into his ear and it will definitely get him in the mood for more dirty talk. You can then expand the phrases by telling your man exactly what you want him to do. The finest dirty talk is when you use verbal descriptions that create pleasurable fantasies in his head. You want to make sure that he cannot get you out of his head.

During your dirty talk in bed make sure you talk about yourself and what you like. There is no need to be shy. You should also talk about him and how he makes you feel. Compliment him. If he is a good kisser you should tell him. If he returns the compliment then it might be a good moment to say something naughty to him.

Dirty talk is about trusting and being trusted because you are being brave and putting yourself in a vulnerable position. It is also about listening to your man and responding to his needs. Find out what he wants to hear. If you are afraid of saying anything wrong then listening to him is extremely important. You have to be a terrific dirty listener before you can become a terrific dirty talker.

One of the easiest ways to talk dirty in bed is simply describing what both of you are doing to each other and how it makes you feel. For instance, if your guy is stroking your breasts, you can simply describe the sensations you feel on your nipples. You could also tell him how warm and firm his hands feel on your breasts and how much you have been longing to feel his hot body on yours all day. Some guys get turned on just by you describing how horny he is making you feel. This type of guy takes great pleasure in knowing that he is giving pleasure to his girl.

When you are talking dirty to your man you have to be true to yourself. If you are not the type to curse like a hard core porn star then there is no need to pretend to be one. However if you are the type that can comfortably switch roles from gentle dirty talk to hardcore dirty talk then there is no need to limit yourself to one type of role. As you become more skilled you could experiment with some hotter role-play activities. Indeed dirty talk is all about expressing yourself. You do not have to pretend to be "goody two shoes" when what you really want to do is to let go of your inhibitions and explore your wild side!

There are times during your love making and dirty talk that your bloke might say things that make you feel uncomfortable. The best thing to do is to pick a time when he is in a relaxed and playful mood to discuss it. It does not have to be on the day. Still it is best to discuss it as soon as possible. In the end your relationship is all about love and respect.

Action Step

First jot down adjectives which you think sound seductive. Some examples are passionate, warm, sultry, aroused, horny, red-hot, eager, sensual, moist, drenched, dripping, soaked, huge, and stiff.

Next jot down verbs which you think sound seductive. Some examples are caress, snuggle, stimulate, stroke, finger, arouse, screw, fuck, excite, fondle, melt, give, rub, pamper, play and lick.

Lastly jot down nouns that you think sound seductive. Some examples are have sex, bed, kiss, taste, nape, hug, waist, hump, embrace, breast, love, intercourse, cuddle, darling, baby, coddle, and sweetheart.

Now pick an adjective, verb and noun that you just jotted down. Connect all three words into a dirty phrase which you feel comfortable using on your lover. You could use them to make up an example phrase like the one below.

Darling stroke my red-hot pussy now.

Darling stroke and tease me, I am so horny for you.

Chapter Six: Sexting

Sexting is the art of using text messages to send sensual messages, pictures and videos to your man on your cell phone. It is created by joining the two words – sex and texting. Sexting has become very popular in recent years with the increasing use of smart phones. The main advantage of Sexting over phone sex is that you can use it anywhere without the fear of being overheard. Sexting used to be mainly used by horny teenagers to express themselves to their heartthrob. How times have changed. Now it is all the rage among adults.

The Smartphone has become an indispensable part of our lives. Indeed I feel completely lost if I do not have mine with me. How else am I going to communicate with the world? Of course I do not have to tell you that the Smartphone has many uses. I use mine to log into Twitter and Facebook, make purchases online, check my bank account, listen to my favorite music collections, and snap my holiday photos and film videos.

For me the most important benefit of my Smartphone is that it enables me to stay in contact with my man in ways that was not even possible a few short years ago. Using my Smartphone to sext my man has been one of the best ways to keep the fires burning in our relationship when we are away from each other for weeks.

The best thing about Sexting is that I can text my man from anywhere. Sending a sext to my lover is so discreet. I can send my lover dirty texts while I am shopping, during a meeting, in the gym or at my hairdresser. I use my cell phone to send dirty text messages to him all the time.

Guess what? I do not just use it for dirty text messages. I also use my cell phone to send semi nude pictures and sexy videos of myself to my guy. In these videos I get into all sorts of naughty activities for his eyes only. He will be left in no doubt of the role-play activities we will engage in when he comes back from overseas.

Using Sexting to send dirty text messages is definitely one of the ways to liven up your relationship. Make sure you use Sexting for foreplay. Appeal to his senses, desires, and emotions. How good you make him feel. How much he wants to touch, taste and smell you. How much he wants to feel your body next to his. How much he wants to make hot sweet love to you. Is he into lingerie?

Make him experience all these desires and emotions through your explicit dirty text messages. Make all his senses tingle in anticipation of holding, smelling, and tasting you. Tease him and get him to think of you all the time. Sexting your lover is just like those old love letters we used to write on paper. I love to relax in my bedroom and read all my old sext messages. The main advantage of Sexting your lover is that you can receive instant replies from him.

I hope you are now convinced that Sexting your partner is one of the most powerful tools in your dirty talking arsenal. You can begin Sexting your partner at any stage in your relationship.

The fantastic thing about using your cell phone to sext your partner is that you become the movie star and central figure in the continuing love story between you and your lover. The best part is that it is actually a true love story being created by both of you. By using text, pictures and video when Sexting, you succeed in making your partner intensely aware of you with his whole mind and body in a way that no porn star will ever do.

If you fancy uniforms, how about sending him sexy pictures of you dressed up in a French maid outfit or in a bunny girl's costume?

Sending dirty text messages is one of the most useful ways to find out what your lover likes in bed. You learn about his interests and fantasies without the awkwardness of talking face to face. For you to maintain a happy relationship you need to work at it to keep the love flames burning. Sending sext messages to your man helps you build an emotional connection with him. Send him teasing messages with explicit details of how horny you will make him when you are together.

Go with your emotions when you sext your partner. Keep it simple and be direct. Make sure you add cute emoticons and smiley faces to express your desire. Text to tell him about the sexy underwear you are wearing. Text him while masturbating to give him a filthy commentary. Text him about how much you love his manly smell. Text to tell him you will spray his favorite fragrance for him to smell on your skin. Send a text telling him how sexy he makes you feel. Ask him what he is thinking.

Here are a couple of examples of what to include in your sext messages.

Luv Ur body.

Ur the best lover ever!

Luv the way U touch my rack.

I'm touching myself all over while thinking about U.

I will not be wearing any underwear for U tonight.

I've a new toy for U to try out on me.

I need every inch of U inside me tonight.

I get so wet thinking about U.

U can do anything U want to me tonight.

I'm dressed up in nurses' uniform and waiting to give you some TLC.

I want to run my hands through Ur sexy goatee.

Tell me what U want; I'm Ur sex slave.

To become a great dirty talker you need to develop your Sexting skills! You will learn more about your man's fantasies and desires in a fun and relaxing manner when you text him. Sending dirty texts to your man regularly helps you become a more confident person and expressive person in bed. It helps you build a strong bond with him in today's busy world.

Kate's Story

My friend Kate was feeling that the romance had gone out of her relationship. She had been with her man Gary for 4 years and felt that they were drifting apart. They were building separate businesses and the stress was taking a taking a toll on their relationship. The worst part was they were not making time to spend some quality time together.

I advised Kate that they had to start spending quality time together. I suggested she could employ a part time worker if she could afford it. This would allow her spend more time with Gary.

I also advised her to rebuild her emotional connection to Gary. I recommended that Sexting Gary was her quickest way to rebuild her emotional connection to him.

Kate was sceptical but decided to give Sexting a try. She started Sexting Gary regularly. At first she concentrated on just telling him how good he made her feel. As he got more responsive to her text messages they started exchanging steamier text messages. They even started sending each other sexy videos of themselves!

In the end they rekindled their love for each other. They both realized that the most important part of their relationship was doing fun things together and being there for each other.

Dangers of Sexting

One major worry with Sexting is the fear that your sexy pictures and videos may get spread all over the Internet. This is less of a worry when you are in a stable relationship with a guy you trust. If you just started going out with your man I advise that you do not start sending semi nude pictures of yourself until you trust him to keep them private.

Action Step

When you are alone record how you sound when you talk dirty on your smart phone. How sexy is your voice when you talk dirty? How confident is your voice when you give commands to your partner. Keep practising until you feel that your voice has become sexier and more confident.

Start sending your lover some sexy text messages. These messages should appeal to his senses, desires, and emotions. The more messages you send the better you will become at Sexting.

Phone sex used to be a quite popular and expensive pastime. That was the case before the increasing widespread use of Sexting. Many a teenager used to run up their parents phone bills calling 900 and 910 numbers to talk dirty. Dirty Phone talk is still a fantastic way to learn how to talk dirty because of its intimate nature. Exchanging dirty talk with your man by phone is very useful in long distance relationships where you are unable to connect to each other by Sexting.

Dirty phone talk is one of the ways for you to spice up your sex life. If you are a shy person and feel uncomfortable about talking dirty face to face then this is a good way to learn to talk dirty.

Phone sex skills are quite similar to the skills you need for dirty text messages. The main difference is that with phone sex calls you require a more private place to make your calls so that people do not overhear you.

Make sure that you only make your phone sex calls to your man when you are relaxed. Do whatever it is that gets you into the mood. This way you are able to express yourself freely on the phone. When you are new to talking dirty on the phone it is best for you to talk about whatever makes both you and your man feel sexy. You do not need to over think what you want to say.

Inspire his fantasies when you are talking to him. Lovemaking begins in the brain and good dirty phone talk to your man will get him yearning to touch and hold you. Make your voice as sexy as possible when talking dirty. This is very important when you are describing how you are going to fulfil his sexual fantasies in bed. A sexy voice filled with passion and desire will ensure that he gets so excited that he can't wait to get his hands on you!

If it your first time talking dirty to your man then you might not be sure what to say. A good place to start is complimenting him about how good he makes you feel in bed. Describe what he does that makes you feel so good in your bedroom. Tell him how it makes you feel. Guys do like compliments no matter how macho they act.

Once your man has gotten warmed up by your sexy talk then it is the right time to ask him what he will like you to do in bed. You should also tell him what you want in bed.

Now I know that some men can be quite uncomfortable about expressing their fantasies. Do not let that worry you. You are both not going to become expert dirty talkers overnight able to express your fantasies without any inhibitions. It will take a little time for both of you to become comfortable enough to say what you want without any fear of being judged.

Tell him what you will wear when you are in bed together. Don't be brief. Give him a detailed description of your sexy lingerie. Tell him how much you want to feel his hands on your lingerie and on your body. If you are not going to be wearing anything when you meet tell him in your most sexy voice.

Masturbate while he is on the phone and make sure that he hears you moaning. Describe what you are doing to him and tell him you can't wait for him to come and take it. Tell him how wet you are. Tell him how furiously you are rubbing your clit and how slippery your pussy feels from all the dripping juices. Describe the sensations that you feel all over your body as your breath quickens in tune with your building orgasm. Tell him how much sweat is dripping off you as you jam your dildo in and out of your pussy.

Do not hold back the passion and sheer hunger of naked lust in your voice. Unless he is made of stone you will have him trembling with desire. The image of your sexy body will be imprinted in his head and he won't be able to stop thinking about you. He will yearn for your womanly scent and body.

Once you become more confident you should up the ante. How about some more phone teasing? You already know some of his role-play fantasies. Now is the time to bring his sexual fantasies to life. What does he fancy? Does he fancy some doctor and nurse dirty talk, Goddess worship, teacher and student dirty talk or boss and secretary dirty talk? It is up to both of you. This is your chance to make him so filled with desire for you that he will have eyes only for you.

Action Step

Call your man on your house telephone. Compliment him and tell him about how wonderful he makes you feel. Tell him how much you long to spend some romantic time with him where you will each fulfil one fantasy. The key is to start with a simple fantasy. As he gets used to your fantasy games you can introduce wilder fantasies to him.

Chapter Eight: Cybersex and Sex Chat Rooms

By now you have become more confident with your dirty talking skills in your bedroom. Are you ready for more talk practice with an advanced dirty talking method? If you are then it means that you are ready for Cybersex. I have to warn you that this type of sexual activity is only for brave souls because you might witness sexual activities that you find shocking,

Cybersex also known as Internet sex is a type of kinky sex activity performed over the internet where two or more persons chat and send each other dirty sex messages. You have to be logged in on the Internet. You can talk dirty during a cybersex session and engage in fantasy sex. During cybersex you and your man can both describe your feelings, desires and actions to each other so that you both get turned on.

Cybersex is commonly performed in sex chat rooms and instant messaging systems. Your sex chat occurs in real time in cyberspace and you can get instant responses to your demands.

Cybersex is best practiced when you and your man are already comfortable with talking dirty to each other. It is an excellent way to make your some of your sexual fantasies come true.

Connecting to your man in cyberspace is also a great way to maintain an intimate long distance relationship. All you need to do is use your webcam and microphone to see and chat to him in real time. You can also engage in a long distance dirty talk masturbation session with him!

When using instant messaging systems for cybersex, you could leave him a message if he is not logged on. In addition, you can record your cybersex session with your man. By recording your session you can always relive them again. Instant messaging systems also enable you save your chat text conversations.

This gives you the chance to read them again in your spare time. Reading them again helps you become a better dirty talker. In today's world, cybersex can also be assessed from smart phones.

The reality is that even though couples love each other they sometimes want other types of sexual experiences. Some couples fantasize about making love to other couples. Other couples fantasize about making love while other people are watching. There are so many sexual activities which appear in couples fantasies.

Cybersex gives you the opportunity to experience these activities in the company of your man. From the safety of your bedroom you can experience virtual sex with other people by talking dirty and acting out your sexual fantasies. Make sure that you both discuss and agree before you try Cybersex.

When you visit a sex chat room you will find both exhibitionist and voyeurs. Exhibitionists love making love to their man while other people are watching. While voyeurs love watching others having sex.

There are always lots of different role-play activities happening in a sex chat room. Most fantasy sex activities that you dream of usually happen in sex chat rooms. You will find people with different sexual fetishes.

Visiting a sex chat room is a fantastic way to practice your dirty talk. When you visit a sex chat room you can remain anonymous and hide your identity by choosing a permanent username. Once you are logged on you can watch and participate in the sex chats. It is a fantastic way to practice your dirty talk and you can choose not to engage in any of the sexual role-play activities.

Next I will tell you about the benefits and dangers of Cybersex.

Benefits of Cybersex

Helps you achieve your sexual fantasies from the safety and comfort of your bedroom.

Helps you practice your dirty talk on others before trying it out on your man.

Dangers of Cybersex

You could become addicted to cybersex and find it difficult to maintain a normal relationship.

You could get sexually involved and have a real life physical affair with the men and women you meet in sex chat rooms and this might end your relationship with your current man.

There is a danger that someone might record your sex session and post it on the Internet.

BDSM involves a lot hard core dirty talk and sexual fantasies. BDSM is a range of kinky and erotic practices which involve role-playing, bondage and discipline, sadism and masochism, dominance and submission, restraint and other interpersonal relationships.

Here is the full meaning of BDSM.

B stands for bondage (This is one the common fantasies in BDSM)

D stands for Dominance

S stands for Submission

M stands for Masochism (usually involves pain)

Most people wrongly think that BDSM is all about pain. This is not actually true in practice. A lot of BDSM activities don't involve pain. Many people also believe that BDSM activities actually increase violence against women. This is not the case as the studies carried out in various countries have not confirmed it. In reality, Japan a country well known for its widespread BDSM activities, has one of the lowest rate of sexual crimes of all developed countries.

A lot of BDSM activities are just about power exchange. Examples of activities involving power exchange include dominance & submission (D&S), and bondage and dominance (B&D). Many men and women find the idea of bondage very erotic. Bondage usually involves tying your partner. Indeed Bondage is one the common fantasies in BDSM.

Many BDSM activities include different types of play. Sexual role-play is a very popular type of play in BDSM.

Here are some hardcore play activities you can practice with your man. You can use them to start practising your dirty talk and exploring some of your sexual fantasies.

Types of Play

Sexual Role-play

This usually involves you playing an erotic sexual fantasy with your man. Here are some scenarios you can practice with your man.

Ageplay (role-play where you treat your partner as either much older or younger than you)

Authority figure play e.g. boss and secretary, teacher and student

Medical play e.g. doctor and nurse, doctor and patient, nurse and patient

Uniform fetishes play e.g. waitress uniform, fireman uniform, prison warden uniform, stripper etc

Gender play (you the female pretend to be the male)

Goddess worship play (your man treats you as his Goddess)

Prison fetish plays e.g. prisoner and warden, prisoner and wardress, prisoner and doctor

Strap on play

Bondage

Soft Spanking

Soft Whipping

Equipment you could use for your Dirty Talk during your BDSM sessions:

Handcuffs

Bondage cuffs

Ropes

Chains

Blindfolds

Soft Whips (for fondling)

Sex Toys e.g. dildos, vibrators and wands

During any BDSM activity with your man it is very important that you use safe words. Safe words prevent both of you from going further than you intended.

BDSM Parties and Clubs

You can go to a BDSM party or club if you are interested in exploring the BDSM scene. During the party you can play with your man in an erotic atmosphere. These types of events are becoming more popular because it gives you the chance to use a wider variety of 'playing equipment' than is usually available in your home. There are BDSM clubs in most of the major cities.

Chapter Ten: Dirty Talk Examples

In previous chapters you learnt how to talk dirty. Now comes the fun part. Some dirty talk examples!

You might be a narrator ("You are running your hands through my hair. Now you are kissing me on my nipples.") Or you might be an affirmation person ("Yeah! Yeah! Yeah! Yeah baby!") Or you might just be the bad girl ("Wow this cucumber feels really good").

I have included many similar illustrations of the dirty talk examples given above. Take a look at them to decide what types of dirty phrases you feel comfortable using on your lover. Study and practice them. The reason that I included these phrases is because a lot of women are not sure what to say when they first start talking dirty to their man.

Be natural when talking dirty to your guy. Try and think of creative phrases that fit his personality. The phrases given in this book are just a guide to get you talking dirty. Remember it is best to make up your own because no one else knows your partner like you do. The most important thing I hope you learn from this book is to practice what you have learnt.

Now some of you might say that some of the dirty talk examples given here are very hardcore. My reason for including them is that I believe that you have the right to decide which dirty talk examples you choose to use in your love life. Don't shoot the messenger for including some hardcore dirty talk examples. This is a dirty talk book after all. LOL!

1. I am 3 times a lady. We are going to do it 3 times tonight.

2. There is going to be an earthquake in bed tonight and we will reach 10 on the Richter scale.

3. You are my prince. Your sexual demands are my pleasure to give.

4. Let's get into the shower together skin to skin and bump and grind to the tempo of the splashing water.

5. Come and open the door to my secret garden. I'm ready to let you in.

6. Your my prince, I am your princess, forget the royal niceties. I want it fast and furious like a sex starved peasant girl.

7. Tonight I will make you rise like a genie in a bottle.

8. Tell me I am your sex goddess. Tell me how much you love, cherish and need me.

9. Big daddy. Your hot sexy French maid needs some sexual healing tonight.

10. I want your hands and lips to explore every inch of my body. Show me that I am your special lady.

11. I am your diva and you better be strong and ready for the demands I will be making tonight.

12. I have a dirty secret to tell you before we go inside the restaurant. I am not wearing any panties under this short skirt.

13. I am going to twerk so hard on your body that you will go faint with desire.

14. Our midnight sex is going to be hotter than you've ever had before. I'm talking steamy, sweat dripping down your back, neighbors pounding on our walls.

15. I want to feel your sexy tongue digging into my hot moist pussy.

16. You are my sunshine and moonlight and you are definitely rocking my world right here in bed.

17. Gosh my nipples are so hard that they hurt. I wish that you were here to suck them for me (text message).

18. Thanks for the flowers baby. Tonight our bodies will be entwined with the scent of the flowers as we make sweet love.

19. We will be making sweet music between the sheets this weekend break. Our bodies will be pounding to the beat of our natural rhythm (phone conversation).

20. Come to my love garden and your sex goddess will grant you all your wishes.

21. I'll be wearing nothing but a Victoria's secret panty when you come home.

22. Dear doctor, I am going to wear that sexy outfit you like tonight. Your little patient needs some vitamin sex (Doctor/Patient role-play).

23. I know you like the way I am twerking. There's going to be a lot of bumping and grinding tonight (on the dance floor).

24. I am wearing this sexy skimpy underwear just for you. Wanna check out what is underneath?

25. Guy tonight this MILF will teach you things no girl has ever shown you before.

26. You think you are a big bad wolf. Tonight you will be like putty in my hands.

27. I think this huge dick is ready for milking and I am goner milk it like a cowgirl.

28. You are my love doctor and I need you to give me some sexual healing.

29. What a naughty boy you have been. I am going to spank you all over.

30. This evening you must carry out all my sexual demands. I'm the princess who must be obeyed.

31. Come on big daddy. Daddy's little girl wants to lick some lollipop.

32. Darling behind this calm exterior is a hot sensual woman panting with desire. Can you feel how much my body yearns for you? Take me. Take it take it all!

33. My sexy hunk, I've put on my vibrating toy and here is the remote. You can use it on me during dinner in the restaurant.

34. You don't look so tough now that it is me doing the fucking. Tell me how it feels to be fucked by a woman.

35. You bring out the woman in me the way you caress my face, throat and pussy with your lips.

36. My master your maid awaits your sexual commands.

37. You know I like the way you ride me. You ride me hard just the way I like it.

38. There must be no touching. I'm goner tease you with my body and my lap dancing skills till you will go wild with desire.

39. I want to watch you touch yourself. Touch yourself and tell me how much you missed me.

40. Baby I want it nice and slow at first and then faster as the electricity in our bodies ignites.

41. Oh daddy yes that's the spot. You are the best, I love the way you lick my pussy.

42. Stud your touch drives me so wild that my whole body is on fire and I quiver and vibrate like a vibrating toy.

43. Guy now you tell me "Sorry teacher I am not going to do it again." Well it's too late for that and you are going to suffer the consequences.

44. You're my one weakness and vice. I just can't get enough of you.

45. You make me moan with delight when you do those things to me.

46. Boy you are going to be severely punished. Go to the naughty corner.

47. Oh baby I am so wet. I wanna sit on your cock and ride you like a horse.

48. Hey boy. I am going to tie you up and have my way with you. You are going to do exactly as I say.

49. I'm the little mermaid that will make all your sexual wishes come true.

50. Tell me how much you want to taste me. Tell me how much you want to taste my honey pot.

51. I am wearing a sexy blue bra and my firm breasts are straining hard against them. You will like to bury your face in them while I jerk you off wouldn't you (telephone conversation)?

52. Yes hunk, fuck me faster. Smack that ass.

53. I have been dreaming of your dong all day. My nipples are as hard as rocks and I wish you were here.

54. You bring out the woman in me with the things you do to me.

55. I'm goner make you beg and yearn for my feminine touch later on.

56. Oh yes you have to beg for it. I know you want some of my creamy pussy juice in your mouth.

57. There's goner be a rumble in our bed tonight.

58. I'm a BBW and tonight I am going to give you more than you can handle.

59. Hey Adonis. I am going to show you that I am the boss tonight. Guess what? You're going to like it.

60. I'm a sexy cougar and your hard young body is here for my pleasure.

61. I must confess that I have been a very bad girl and I'm going to need some spanking.

62. I'm goner make love to you again and again all night long.

63. Guy I've been watching you like a hawk in the sky all day and I want you for my supper.

64. I'm the goddess of love and will grant you all your sexual wishes tonight.

65. Hold me tight I want to feel your heart beating next to mine. I want to feel your hard body melt into mine.

66. I'm a demanding madam. All my demands must be promptly met or you will be severely punished.

67. My temperature keeps rising and rising and I need some sexual relief.

68. I can see you like me in my stable girl clothes. Well I plan to ride you tonight.

69. My dear I need some of your long candy inside me.

70. Oh yeah it feels so nice when you suck my toes. Keep moving those lips up my body.

71. Don't you dare cum boy until I tell you or you will be sorry you disobeyed my command.

72. Take off your clothes beefcake. I want to do it right here in the grass with you.

73. Dude there is no place to run. I have hidden the bedroom key and you are not leaving until I have had my fill.

74. Tie me up hunk and take me.

75. Come-on stud. Push those buttons that make me behave like a tramp.

76. I love the things you do with your mouth all over me.

77. Strap up and get down on your hands and knees guy. I am goner ride you like a pony.

78. Kiss me all over from my head down to the tip of my boot heels.

79. Lay back big daddy and brace yourself. I'm ready to rev you up.

80. Happy birthday, I'm all covered in cake from jumping out from your giant birthday cake. Lick me up from head to toe.

81. Darling it was mind-blowing. It's the greatest fuck we've ever had.

82. I am going to be your geisha girl for tonight. First of all I will wine and dine you and after that you can have me for dessert.

83. I am going to give you a midnight examination in my skimpy nurse's uniform.

84. I want you for dessert because you're the only healthy dessert I know.

85. You want to know what I am wearing. Well I am wearing lovely black stockings with suspenders. My panties are soaking wet and I can't stop thinking about you (phone conversation).

86. Smack it daddy. I belong to you.

87. You have been a very bad boy today. Bend down and take your punishment from your mistress.

88. Stud I feel so thirsty. I need some of your sexy smoothie.

89. I can't stand it any longer. Lie back and let me ride you like the slut you know that I am.

90. Run your lips all over my body hunk and make sure you get the soles of my feet nice and wet.

91. When you wave your magic wand like that I get all wet inside.

92. Glad you came home early. Forget dinner and let's get down to some naughty business.

93. I'm the sexy girl who will give you the kind of mind blowing sex that will shatter the Richter scale.

94. I need a roughneck to satisfy me this evening.

95. I am going to stroke, suck, sip, taste and tease you until you beg for more.

96. I've been a bad girl and I've been stealing glances at the crotch of men's trousers all day. Give me the real thing right now.

97. You're my Jack and I'm your Jill. Let's fetch some water for fun and then fall into bed for some splashing, tumbling, rolling and frolicking.

98. Taste my pussy baby. It is dripping wet and craving for the warmth of your mouth.

99. Daddy's little girl wants to play with the hot magic wand.

100. I'm addicted to your touch. Let's have a roll in the hay in the farmhouse barn.

101. Spread the whipped cream and chocolate on my body and have a feast.

102. Hey toyboy. Tonight I am going to give you so much pleasure that you will keep coming back to mama.

103. My body is telling me yes. I want to feel every inch of you on my body.

104. Your tongue right there. It makes me feel so good.

105. I can't wait for you to operate with your magic touch and give me some instant relief.

106. You dirty boy… you'd just love it if I fucked you with this dildo. Well if you beg me I might make your wishes come true.

107. You know how to do it right. You make me feel complete when you touch me.

108. Wake up, wake up, wake up! Baby get up I need your midnight love medicine to relieve me.

109. I can't hold it much longer. It's getting stronger and stronger and the O is about to go splash!

110. Your warm hard body feels like a sleek sports car. I want to grab your lever and rev you up.

111. Lie back and let me do to you what no other girl has ever done to you before... take you to ecstasy and beyond!

112. I wish you could drop some ice on my hot breasts and suck the water off my hot erect nipples.

113. Do you like the way my hips push up the water in the pool? Umm there might be some hip action for us tonight.

114. Baby I am thinking about what I would like for desserts. Well I will like something long, hot and filling.

115. It is going to get hot and steamy in the Jacuzzi tonight and I do not just mean from the water!

116. Yes darling I am relaxing in the Jacuzzi. Wow these power jets are giving me so much pleasure and remind me of you.

117. Play my body like a flute hunk. Up down up down!

118. Stud, I am going to explore every inch of you with my tongue.

119. Umm your tongue feels wonderful down there. Up, down, left, and right, this is ecstasy.

120. I am going to ride you hard. I am not goody two shoes butter won't melt in her mouth.

121. Oh big daddy. Your little princess needs some sexual healing.

122. I feel like a bitch in heat. You better get home quick because I can't wait any longer (text message).

123. I have seen the way you look at my behind when I bend over to open the kitchen cupboards. I am on all fours now on the living room rug. Come and get it (text message).

124. Leave the lights on, turn up the air conditioner and take everything off me. It's about to get hot and steamy in here.

125. I can see that you are bulging in your trousers. Well I have a nursing remedy for that when we get home.

126. I am masturbating and panting with desire. Can you hear the sound of my juices in my cunt? I wish you were here so that I could squirt all over you (smart phone conversation).

127. Sissy boy tonight your body is mine. Your lips and tongue must obey my pussy commands.

128. Remember the Arabian night tales. Tonight I am going to give you a thousand and one pleasures in one night with my body.

129. I have tricks in my kitty that will make a Geisha girl blush.

130. Wow it's so sunny on the beach today and my fanny is tingling. Let's have some oral action in the icy waters.

131. You deserve a little spanking dirty boy. As your punishment you are going to fulfill every dirty demand I make.

132. I love the way you kiss me from my head down to my foot soles.

133. Gigolo my honeycomb is ready for harvesting. Come and sip some of my honey.

134. Say my name hunk. Tell me how no girl can ever do the dirty like I do.

135. I'm your million dollar girl and I have some gifts for you that no other girl has ever given you.

136. Ooh daddy, I'm hot like an oven. Go down on me and quench all these fires burning inside me.

137. You are like a sleek Rolls Royce. Get ready to have your engine revved up!

138. I want you to make love to me in the rain. In this soft long grass with the sweet earth smell filling our nostrils.

139. Make love to me behind the trees in the park. I don't care who is watching.

140. I'm a sex diva and when I get these urges I demand that you satisfy me!

141. I'm the good girl who has turned bad. And I am going to tie you up and unleash my lusts on you.

142. I want to fill our Jacuzzi in champagne. Then we will jump in and make sweet love.

143. I've been thinking of it all day and I just gotta have it.

144. Let's forget about food and do it on this table.

145. Faster, faster bad boy. You are the daddy.

146. So what do you fancy for role play tonight, Cinderella or the sex starved prison wardress?

147. I love being such a slut. It makes me feel complete.

148. My mind is saying no but my body is saying yes. Come take control of my mind and body.

149. Tell me all the naughty things you fantasize about when you think of me. Do not leave anything out.

150. Your wishes are my pleasure. Tell me what you desire.

151. There is a storm igniting inside me and I need you at the wheel to bring me to calm waters.

152. Steady my rocking boat. Quench all these hot passions flowing inside me.

153. Let's lie down on the waterbed and give in to our lust and passion.

154. I will do anything you want but I will only grant you three sexual wishes.

155. Boyfriend you know how to get me all primed up and ready with your touch. I am ready to erupt like a surface to air missile.

156. I will be in leather and lace just for you tonight.

157. It's just the two of us tonight. It will be caviar, champagne, candlelight and Jacuzzis.

158. You are going to be the genie in my fanny tonight.

159. I am the bad girl who gets you in a twist and I am saving the best for the last.

160. You are my first and my last and tonight we are goner make an earthquake in bed.

161. I've got something in mind for a midnight snack, skinny dipping and then making love on the warm beach sand.

162. Turn off the lights, light a candle, its love by candlelight.

163. I've got something in store for you tonight that is for your eyes only.

164. My shining star there is going to be fireworks in bed tonight.

165. Tonight we celebrate our love with champagne and caviar and love of the fast and furious kind.

166. I am going to be your kitty cat tonight but I warn you that I'm a tigress when touched the right way.

167. When you come back I will have nothing on except for strawberries and whipped cream.

168. I know I'm old enough to be your mum but I've got tricks in my milkshake that will make you hungry for more.

169. You just can't keep your eyes off my booty... hmm the main course is tonight.

170. We'll take a ride on the lake in the gondola and then find a hidden cove to make love.

171. You are my kryptonite and you know how to me feel weak with desire.

172. I feel thirsty. Come here and let me have some of your love elixir.

173. You will groan with pleasure all night from the things I will do to you.

174. Fling off my sexy beachwear and make love to me in the blue lagoon.

175. My master my body awaits in quivering anticipation. I am ready to satisfy your every wish and desire.

176. I am your sex goddess. Even Venus has nothing to compare to the pleasures that I have in store for you.

177. Dude tonight I will make you so horny that you will keep saying my name.

178. When you press those buttons on me I become a tigress and hunter.

179. I am going to be your geisha girl all night long.

180. Come quickly I am inside the beach hut and I'm only wearing a Victoria secret's V-string panty.

181. It will be just the two of us. You will find out that I am not the good girl you seem to think that I am.

182. Can you see how hard my nipples are in my tight fitting t-shirt? It needs your lips and some ice.

183. You unleash my passions and bring out the lioness in me. With you I am not daddy's little girl.

184. You make me feel complete and bring out the horny girl in me.

185. I want us to meet for a late night rendezvous at our secret place and we will be doing more than holding hands and whispering sweet endearments (role-play).

186. I am going to wine and dine you. Our main course is each other.

187. This is just the way I like it. You are hitting the spot right there and making me lose control of my senses.

188. I will make our bodies beat in tempo to the music and our passions will rise to a crescendo (text message).

189. All I smell is your manly body and the smell of roses. Take me now on this garden lawn in the rain.

190. Let our bodies move together in rhythm. You can play any beat you want on my body to raise the tempo of my libido.

191. Big daddy tonight is not a Cinderella love night. It is sweat dripping from our bodies' hot sex.

192. Stud it is goner be like a boxing bout in bed tonight.

193. You bring out the tigress in me and tonight you are my prey.

194. Meow. Stud this kitty cat needs some of your milk.

195. I love the way this cucumber feels in my hands. It reminds me of you. I can nibble it, eat it or slide it in (Smartphone conversation).

196. Going bowling with you is so much fun and I love the way you hit the head pin every time. I know you will be hitting the spot that makes me gush tonight.

197. We will both play Romeo and Juliet tonight just the two of us. Our version will be steamier and raunchier.

198. Naughty boy you have not done your homework. Bend over I am going to spank you (Female teacher/male student role-play).

199. Dude I am all hot and horny. I want you to play me like a tambourine tonight.

200. Plus you I am whole. Minus you I'm nothing.

Terms you can use to describe yourself

Tart, hooker, slag, slut, tramp, prostitute, harlot, wanton, bitch, hussy, wench, dame, madam, queen, mistress, Jezebel, floozie, floozy, wanton, hoe, trash, little girl, naughty girl, dirty girl

Terms you can use to describe your guy

Gigolo, baby, hottie, heart-throb, beefcake, hunk, cutie, sexy beast, Adonis, beast, guy, lady-killer, super stud, big daddy, royal stud, boss, master, daddy

Action step

Take a look at the dirty talk phrases examples in this chapter. Write down the ones that you feel comfortable using. Next add some of your own phrases to the phrases you picked from this book. Practice these dirty talk phrases on your own until you feel comfortable using them on your partner. Make sure you practice them aloud.

Also look at the "terms you can use to describe yourself" and "terms you can use to describe your guy". Decide which terms you feel comfortable using so that you can add them to your dirty talk vocabulary.

Chapter Eleven: Resources Guide

Sex is not just about talking dirty. I believe that women should know more about their bodies. Indeed better knowledge of our bodies helps us feel more confident about talking dirty. Sexual knowledge is also about looking after ourselves. Taking care of our bodies also keeps us healthy and happy. This is why I have decided to include some useful information in this section.

The remaining part of this book is the resource guide section. I have provided you with a dirty talk toolbox in the resource guide section. Here you will learn more about your female sexual body. You will also find out about an exercise called Kegel exercise. This exercise helps you tone your pelvic muscles. Practising Kegel exercises will help you achieve stronger orgasms. You will also find the sex toys section, sex toys care section and reputable adult sex shop addresses section.

Dirty Talk Toolbox

In this section we will talk about female genitalia, Kegel exercises, sex toys care, sex toys for masturbation and adult sex shops. I will also tell you about some female ejaculation misconceptions and give you some G-spot and squirting tips.

First you will learn about your female sexual anatomy. The more you learn about your body the more enjoyment you obtain from sex. Understanding your female anatomy helps you understand how you get sexually aroused.

Female Genitalia – Your Female Sexual Anatomy

Here you will find out about your vulva, anus and PC muscles.

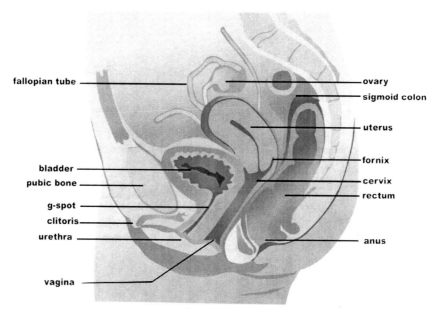

Vulva

Your vulva includes all your external female genitalia including your vagina, clitoral gland and hood, urethral opening, inner and outer labia, and your pubic mound. Indeed your vulva is different from those of other women! Here is a brief description of each of the major parts.

Pubic Mound

Your pubic mound is the mass of fatty tissue positioned over the pubic bone. It is usually covered with pubic hair.

Labia

Your inner and outer labia are extremely sensitive to touch and stimulations. When you become extremely aroused, they might both swell and change colour.

Clitoral gland and hood

Your clitoral gland is what you usually call the clitoris and is part of your clitoral structure. The clitoris is one of your most sensitive body parts. It is highly pleasurable to touch and stimulation and is the external part of your clitoral shaft.

Your clitoral gland and shaft become erect when you are highly aroused. Once this happens your clitoris will retreat under the clitoral hood.

The Vagina

Your vagina consists of a canal which starts at the vaginal opening. At the inner end of the canal is the cervix. When you are aroused your vaginal walls swell and produce lubrication. Sometimes you might be highly aroused but your vagina might not create enough lubrication to make penetration comfortable! This is where gels and lubricants are quite useful.

The Urethra

Above the opening to the vagina is your urethral opening. The urethral opening is where urine exits your body. The urethra is the internal tube that leads to the bladder. It is surrounded by spongy erectile tissue called the urethral sponge.

Part of the urethral sponge can be felt through the front wall of the vagina (about 2.5cm to 5cm inside the vagina). This area of the vagina with the urethral sponge behind it is the famous G-spot.

When you are aroused your urethral sponge becomes erect. You will find it very pleasurable stimulating your G-spot when your urethral sponge becomes erect. When I get highly aroused and my urethral sponge is properly stimulated I sometimes ejaculate! This is the famous squirting or female ejaculation.

The Anus

The anus is the opening to your anal canal and rectum. Your anal canal consists of soft and sensitive tissues and muscles. Beyond the anal canal is your rectum. The rectum is about 8 to 9 inches long and consists of folds soft and smooth tissue. Your rectum can expand when you are aroused. This makes penetration more likely once you learn to relax your anal muscles.

The PC muscles

The PC muscles are a group of broad flat muscles found at the bottom of your pelvic floor. You will get many benefits when you regularly exercise your PC muscles. These benefits include better bladder control, more pleasurable penetration, better control of your orgasms, and stronger, longer orgasms.

To find your PC muscles, pretend you are peeing and want to stop the flow of urine. The muscles you use are your PC muscles.

There are a set of exercises called Kegel exercises. They are named in honour of the gynaecologist called Arnold Kegel. These exercises help you tone your pelvic muscles.

EXERCISE 1

Make sure you are completely relaxed. Now concentrate on your genitalia. Take a series of strong breaths. Take another strong breath and while you breathe in contract your pelvic muscles. Make sure you hold the contraction for a couple of seconds. You can now exhale and relax your pelvic muscles. Start by doing this between 20 to 30 times. Keep practicing this until you are able to do this about 100 times in one daily session.

EXERCISE 2

Get yourself into a relaxed mood. Again concentrate on your genitalia. Take a series of powerful breaths. Now inhale deeply as you take another breath and make sure you tense and release your muscles continually. Tense and release those muscles about 10 times. You can breathe out and relax. It is best if you do the contractions rapidly. These 10 repetitions will count as one set of exercises. Keep practising until you are able to do 20 to 50 sets daily.

EXERCISE 3

Once you are relaxed concentrate on your genitalia. Take a series of strong breaths. Now while taking another strong breath, contract your pussy and anus as if you are trying to push out an object. Breathe out and thrust while pretending you are pushing out the object. This is also a great exercise for your belly muscles. Do about 20 to 50 repetitions every day.

Female Ejaculation (Squirting) Misconception

Female Ejaculation during masturbation or sex is normal and healthy. Some women ejaculate and feel embarrassed because they feel something is wrong with them. Sometimes they avoid sex or orgasms to prevent themselves from squirting.

The astonishing fact is that some family doctors do not know much about it. Some women who discussed it with their doctors were told they suffered from a medical condition called incontinence. Incontinence sometimes means involuntary urination. You can see why the women were not eager to feel embarrassed during sex. The truth is nothing was wrong with them. They were simply squirting.

G-spot and Female Ejaculation (Squirting) Tips and Guide

1. The G-spot is named after the German gynaecologist Ernest Grafenberg.

2. The G-spot is the source of female ejaculation.

3. The G-spot is much easier to find when you are aroused.

4. Sex toys make it easier to find and stimulate your G-spot than using your fingers.

5. Female ejaculation is normal and healthy.

6. Some girls confuse squirting for involuntary peeing or incontinence.

7. Squirting comes out of the urethra.

8. Some women say that they have never squirted.

9. Exercising your PC muscles may help you squirt better.

10. Make sure you drink lots of liquid as this will help you to squirt during sex or masturbation.

11. Some girls squirt a little while some squirt a lot.

12. It is a good idea to pee before your squirting session.

13. Some women can only ejaculate from clitoral stimulation.

14. Women often describe G-spot orgasms as a deeper orgasm than orgasms from clitoral stimulation. During G-spot orgasms they feel contractions deep in their vaginal walls and uterus.

15. When you get the feeling that you are going to pee during a G-spot session, relax, do not tense your pelvic muscles as this does not help you reach an orgasm.

16. Kegel exercises help you tone your pelvic muscles for better squirting.

17. Some women can orgasm and ejaculate at the same time.

18. Not all women prefer G-spot orgasms, some prefer clitoral orgasms.

Sex Toys for Masturbating

Here are some of the sex toys you can use to spice up your love life. You can use toys to aid you in your dirty talk with your partner during sex.

Lubes or Gels

Lubes or gels are lubricants used during masturbation or sex. There are a wide variety of lubes. These include water based lubes, organic lubes, silicone lubes and hybrid lubes. Using lubes helps you keep your vagina and anus wet during masturbation.

Water Based Lubes

Water based lubes can be light fluids or range from semi light to extremely thick lubes.

Reputable brands include Astroglide, Wet Pink Water, Durex and K-Y Jelly.

There are some flavoured water based lubes. These flavoured ones taste better and include popular brands like ID and System JO.

If you like to keep your genitals warm during masturbation then go for a warming lube. Famous brands include Emerita OH, ID Sensation and Astroglide Warming Liquid. When going for water based lubes it is best to get lubes that are free of glycerin or parabens.

If you prefer organic products then get Organic lubes. They contain more natural chemicals. Well- known brands include Blossom Organics, Aloe Cadabra and Hathor Aphrodisia.

Silicone Lubes

Silicone lubes are usually flavorless and more costly than water based lubes. One advantage of silicone lubes is that they are highly condensed. In comparison to water based lubes you only have to use a small amount. Hence it takes a longer while before you need to buy another silicone lube.

Silicone lubes are fantastic for condoms. They are also excellent for shower or bath use because they remain smooth underwater. Take note that silicone lubes are unsuited for silicone sex toys.

Well-known brands include Wet Platinum, Eros, Swiss Navy, ID Velvet, Euros and Intrigue.

Dildos

Dildos are non-vibrating sex toys made for penetration. These toys are good for G-spot arousal. They come in different shapes and lengths. Some dildos can be used inside the body. Dildos are shaped like a man's penis.

Dildos are great for masturbating. You can use it when you are alone. Make use of them when you are alone and practicing your dirty talk. You can also use it with your man during partnered masturbation.

Some men feel uncomfortable using a dildo on a woman. They feel that it endangers their manhood. Reassure your man it does not take away his manliness. Ask him to use it on you during your dirty talk sex session.

Flexible Dildos

Silicone dildos are durable and easy to clean. A good silicone dildo is the G-Force dildo. It can be disinfected, warms to body temperature, and conducts vibration best.

Silicone is the most expensive of the soft materials, but it's worth it. The main disadvantage is that you cannot use silicone lubricants with toys made of silicone.

If you want to a cheaper dildo, you can buy one made of softened PVC, rubber, thermal plastic or vinyl. However you need to replace these cheaper dildos very often. Make sure you do not share these cheaper dildos with other people.

Strap-on Harnesses for Dildos

Strap-ons are used to enjoy hands-free penetrative sex. It is good for guys that have erection problems. Strap-ons are ideal for your dirty talk and role-play sessions with your man.

Strapon-on dildos and harnesses can sometimes be bought together in shops. Nevertheless it is better for you to buy them separately so that you can choose both the dildo and harness to fit your body build. Harnesses are usually made of rubber, leather, vinyl and nylon.

Harnesses come in two main styles namely one-strap and two-strap harnesses. One-strap harness is usually a good choice for small women.

Two-strap harnesses come in a variety of styles. They are a good choice if you have a smaller or bigger than average dildo.

Wands

Wands are non-vibrating toys made for handheld use. They come in creative shapes curved like a U or an S, or some variation for comfortable insertion. They are usually made of solid or firm materials such as glass, metal, or hard plastic.

Wands are ideal for G-spot stimulation because of their hard surface. The G-spot responds to firm and constant pressure. Because of their high-quality materials, wands tend to be expensive.

Glass Wands

Glass wands come in a variety of shapes and colours. They can also be handmade. Glass wands are very popular. They can be shaped like a glass penis, candy cane, baton, or a curved wand. The main advantage of glass wands is its smoothness and compatibility with all types of lubricants.

Steel Wands

Steel wands are smooth and shiny. They are usually heavier than glass wands and are very durable. They are also easy to clean and compatible with all types of lubes. Steel wands create wonderful sensations during penetration. They are very popular wands. The Pure Epiphora wand is a well-known steel wand.

Plastic Wands

Plastic wands are firm and stiff wands. They are sometimes cheaper than glass and steel wands. Nevertheless they are sometimes quite expensive. Plastic wands can be made of medical grade non toxic plastic, acrylic or Lucite.

Inserted vibrators

Inserted vibrators are great for penetration and G-spot stimulation. They come in different lengths of between 4 inches and 14 inches. Most of them tend to be about 7 to 8 inches.

Some of these vibrators are shaped like penises while other are curved. Inserted vibrators are usually created from silicone, PVC or plastics. Some inserted vibrators can be recharged while others are battery powered. These vibrators are designed for penetration rather than external clitoral stimulation.

Dual-Action Vibrators

Dual-action vibrators are absolutely fantastic sex toys. You can use them for penetration and clitoral stimulation in unison. If you want to enjoy some earth-shattering moments of pleasure these vibrators might just do the trick! There are two main types of dual-action vibrators. These are rabbit style and curved double action.

Rabbit-style Vibrators

Rabbit-style vibrators were made famous by "Sex and the City". They are usually manufactured from elastomer, rubber, silicone, PVC or TPR. These vibrators are normally penis shaped with a clitoral attachment which is usually in the shape of an animal.

Curve shaped rabbit vibrators are also available. There are many variations of rabbit vibrators in the market. If you walk into any reputable sex shop you will be sure to find them.

Curved Double-Action Vibrators

These types of vibrators usually come in U, S and "smile" shapes. Curved Double- Action Vibrators are usually the best vibrators for reaching inside your vagina. It is especially useful for reaching those spots in your vagina you find difficult to reach during masturbation. Needless to say it is excellent for G-spot stimulation. Use it to stimulate your vulva and clitoris simultaneously.

Condoms

Condoms are useful for preventing unwanted pregnancies. Of course you should always contact your doctor to recommend different contraceptives.

There are both lubricated and non-lubricated condoms in the market. Non-lubricated condoms are excellent for oral sex. You can also use flavoured condoms for oral sex. When using condoms it is a good idea to use non-lubricated condoms because you can regulate the amount of lube you use.

Oral Dams

Oral dams are very useful if you're lovemaking usually includes cunnilingus and analingus. They help in preventing infections. Dams are very delicate but yet they are strong. To use it simply dab some lube over the vagina or anus and place the dam on it. Remember to throw it away once you have finished having sex.

Sex Toy Care

My best advice is to follow the manufacturer's recommendations when it comes to cleaning your sex toy.

You can share sex toys made of metal, hard plastic, glass or acrylic with other people. However if you are going to do this make sure you put a condom on the sex toy.

Never share sex toys made of vinyl, jelly, rubber, CyberSkin, PVC or jelly rubber.

ACTION STEP

Go to a woman friendly sex shop to check out and find out more about the toys. If you are shy, you could order online from a trustworthy website. You can also ring some of the adult sex shops with the contact details given in the adult sex shop addresses section.

Chapter Twelve: Conclusion

I hope you are now more confident about your ability to talk dirty. Dirty talk is really about fulfilling you and your lover's sexual needs and fantasies in bed when you make love. It is all about not being afraid to express yourself and show who you really are.

My Special Thanks to You

I am giving you my heartfelt thanks for buying my book. I hope you enjoyed this guide. I have consolidated all my dirty talk knowledge into this guide. It is my sincere wish that you practice what you have learnt in this book. If you practice my suggestions you will definitely become a more confident dirty talker and you will form a deeper emotional connection to your man.

Tell all your girlfriends about this book because it would give me great pleasure if they read it. I will also love to hear from you and will be very grateful if you could leave me a review for this book after reading it.

Please leave a good **Review** on **Amazon** after you have finished reading this book to tell me what you have learnt from this guide.

You can go to the Amazon page

http://www.amazon.com/How-Talk-Dirty-Talking-Examples-ebook/dp/B00JLZDU70

Once you are there click on "Write a review". I will be forever in your debt!

My Website:

My website address is given below. While you are on my website you can subscribe to my newsletter and I will send you regular dirty talk tips. If you subscribe to my newsletter I will also send you a further 100 dirty talk examples!

My website blog address is given below:

http://www.talkingdirtytoyourman.com/blog

--DK Overbaker

Adult Sex Shop Addresses

These are all reputable shops. I have included the addresses of their shops around some of the world's major cities. You can contact them to find out the location of their shops in your local area.

Agent Provocateur

www.agentprovocateur.com

6 Broadwick St

Soho, London

W1F 8HL

+44 (0)20 7439 0229

3rd Floor Selfridges

400 Oxford Street, London

W1A 1AB

+44 (0)800 123400

Harrods

87-135 Brompton Road

Knightsbridge, London

SW1X 7XL

+44 (0)207 730 1234   ext. 3521

213 Ingram Street

Glasgow, G1 1DQ

Scotland

United Kingdom

+44 (0)141 221 2538

Selfridges

1 The Dome

The Trafford Centre, Manchester

M17 8DA

United Kingdom

0161 629 1233

4th Floor Selfridges

Upper Mall East

Bullring, Birmingham

B5 4BP

United Kingdom

+44 (0)121 600 6766

Bloomingdales

Intimate Apparel-4th floor

1000 Third Avenue

New York

NY 10022

+1 212-705-2974

123 Newbury Street

Boston

MA 02116

+1 617 267-0229

Phipps Plaza Mall

Level 1, Monarch Court

3500 Peachtree Road NE

Atlanta

GA 30326

+14048692881

47 East Oak Street

Chicago

IL 60611

USA

+1 312 335 0229

The Forum Shops at Caesars

3500 Las Vegas Boulevard

Suite R18

Las Vegas

NV 89109

USA

+1 702 6967174

242 N. Rodeo Drive

Beverly Hills

CA 90210

+1 310 888 0050

7961 Melrose Avenue

Los Angeles

CA 90046

+1 323 653 0229

9700 Collins Avenue

201, Bal Harbour Shops

Bal Harbour

Miami

FL 33154

+1 305-865-3909

Village of Merrick Park

360 San Lorenzo Ave

Suite 1502

Coral Gables

FL 33146

+1 305 460 0066

Holt Renfrew

50 Bloor Street West

Toronto

ON M4W 1A1

Canada

+1 416 922 2333 ext. 21253

Holt Renfrew

1300 Sherbrooke Street West

Montreal

QC H3G 1H9

+1 514 282 3749

Holt Renfrew

737 Dunsmuir Street

Vancouver

BC V7Y 1E4

+1 604 681 3121

A Little More Interesting

www.alittlemoreinteresting.com

17th Avenue Location

1501B, 17th Ave SW

Calgary AB T2T 0E2, Canada

403 475 7775

Ann Summers

www.annsummers.com

104 Kensington High Street

Kensington, London

W8 4SG

+44 (0)87 0053 4107

Unit 11

35 Palace Gardens Shopping Centre

Enfield, London

EN2 6SN

+44 (0)2032 322163

Unit 21 Lewisham Centre

Lewisham, London

SE13 7EP

+44 (0) 870 0423 2857

522 Oxford Street, London

W1C 1LL

+44 (0)87 0053 4086

104 Oxford Street, London

W1D 1LP

+44(0)87 0053 4042

Su1033 Westfield Shopping Centre

Stratford, London

E20 1EL

+44(0)87 0423 2865

Su 14 Victoria Place Shopping Centre

Victoria, London

SW1W 9SJ

+44(0)87 0053 4094

79 Wardour Street

Soho, London

W1D 6QB

+44(0)87 0053 4011

Unit 53 The Mall

Wood Green, London

N22 6YA

+44(0)87 0423 2860

Aren't We Naughty

www.arentwenaughty.com

1531 Merivale Road, Ottawa, ON,

Canada K2G 3J3

(613) 221-9592

Art of Loving

www.artofloving.ca

1819 West Fifth Avenue

Vancouver, BC

Canada V6J 1P5

604 742 9988

Atsuko Kudo

www.atsukokudo.com

64 Holloway Road

Holloway, London

N7 8JL

+44(0)20 7697 9072

A Woman's Touch

www.a-womans-touch.com

302 S. Livingston St

Madison, WI 53703

608.250.1928

888.621.8880 Toll Free

Babeland

www.babeland.com

707 E Pike St

Seattle

Washington 98122

 206 328 2914

94 Rivington St

New York

New York 10002

212 375-1701

43 Mercer St

New York

New York 10013

212 966 2120

462 Bergen St

Brooklyn

New York 11217

718-638-3820

Coco de Mer

www.coco-de-mer.com

23 Monmouth St

Covent Garden, London

WC2H 9DD

+44(0)12 2531 2077

Come As You Are

www.comeasyouare.com

493 Queen Street West

Toronto, Canada

416-504-7934

Early to Bed

www.early2bed.com

5044 North Clark Street

Chicago, IL 60640

773-271-1219

Forbidden Fruit

www.forbiddenfruit.com

108 E. North Loop

Austin

ATX 78702

1.800.315.2029

Good for Her

www.goodforher.com

175 Harbord Street

Toronto M5S 1H3

Canada

416-588-0900

Good Vibrations

www.goodvibes.com

603 Valencia Street (at 17th Street)

San Francisco, CA 94110

415-503-9522

Harmony

www.harmonystore.co.uk

4 Walkers Court

Soho

London W1F 0BS

+44 (0)20 7287 7345

103 Oxford Street

Oxford Street

London W1D 2HF

+44(0) 20 7734 5969

Madame Liberty

www.madameliberty.com

53 Chandos Place, Covent Garden

London WC2N 4HS

+44(0)78 0865 0100

Passional Boutique

www.passionalboutique.wordpress.com

PASSIONAL Boutique

704 S. 5th Street

Philadelphia PA 19147

215-829-4986

RoB London

www.rob.eu

The Hoist-Arches 47C

South Lambert Road, London

SW8 1RH

 United Kingdom

+44 (0)207 582 5699

Self Serve Toys

www.selfservetoys.com
3904B Central Ave SE

Albuquerque

NM 87108

505-265-5815

Sh! Women's Erotic Emporium

www.sh-womenstore.com

57 Hoxton Square, London

N1 6PD

+44 (0)207 613 5458

Sugar

www.sugartheshop.com

927 West 36th Street

Hampden

Baltimore

MD 21211

410.467.2632

The Pleasure Chest

www.thepleasurechest.com

3436 North Lincoln Avenue

Chicago

IL 60657

773-525-7151

7733 Santa Monica Blvd.

West Hollywood

CA 90046

Los Angeles

323-650-1022

156 Seventh Avenue South

New York

NY 10014

212-242-2158

The Stockroom

www.stockroom.com

2807 W. Sunset Blvd.

Los Angeles

CA 90026

213-989-0334

Tulip

www.mytulip.com

Lakeview

3459 N. Halsted Street

Chicago

Illinois 60657

773-975-1515

1480 W. Berwyn Avenue

Chicago

Illinois 60640

773-275-6110

Ziggla

www.ziggla.com

Fulham Road, London

SW6 5SL

+44 (0)207 384 1862

Reference/Bibliography

University of Granada (2007, June 28). Study Confirms Importance Of Sexual Fantasies In Experience Of Sexual Desire. *ScienceDaily*. Retrieved from

http://www.sciencedaily.com/releases/2007/06/070627223851.htm

Note:

I will be very grateful if you leave me a review. Please leave a good **Review** on **Amazon** after you have finished reading this book to tell me what you have learnt from this guide.

You can go to the Amazon page

http://www.amazon.com/How-Talk-Dirty-Talking-Examples-ebook/dp/B00JLZDU70

Once you are there click on "Write a review". I will be forever in your debt!

My Website:

My website address is given below. While you are on my website you can subscribe to my newsletter and I will send you regular dirty talk tips. Simply enter your name and email in the "Subscribe to our Newsletter" opt in box and I will send you regular dirty talk tips! If you subscribe to my newsletter I will also send you a further 100 dirty talk examples!

My website blog address is given below:

http://www.talkingdirtytoyourman.com/blog

--DK Overbaker

CPSIA information can be obtained at www.ICGtesting.com
Printed in the USA
BVOW04s0317100215

386954BV00036B/484/P